The Old Testament
Made Easy

The Old Testament
Made Easy

Jeanne Steig

pictures by William Steig

MICHAEL DI CAPUA BOOKS

FARRAR · STRAUS · GIROUX · *New York*

For Melinda, Sidonie, Jonas, and Emma

And God Said,
"Let Us Make Man"

"All this in just six days!" God cried.
"I am supremely satisfied.
Those dainty finned and creeping things,
The ones with hooves, the ones with wings!
This world's divine. Just one thing more—
Two-legged, furless omnivore.
Free will, at least to some degree.
The creature quite resembles me.
It only wants a breath of life;
And then, of course, it wants a wife.
No sooner asked, my boy, than done!
They will afford me hours of fun.
See how they blink, and stretch, and grin.
Now let the comedy begin!"

In the Garden

"My darling Rib," said Adam, "please—
It isn't any use to tease.
I don't want fruit. I've just had lunch."
"One bite!" begged Eve. "You'll love the crunch!"

The Invention of Murder

Cain, in a brutish frenzy, rose
And struck his brother dead.
The Lord was moved to fulminate
Upon his wretched head.

"Am I my brother's keeper, then?"
  Cain peevishly inquired.
"You are," said God, "and you have caused
  That brother to expire.

"I set my mark upon your brow.
  You'll find no place to hide.
  Go forth, abhorred by every man,
  O filthy fratricide!"

So Cain went out to dwell in Nod,
  He wedded and begat.
  And Adam sired another son.
"Well, that," said God, "is that."

Methuselah

Insufficiently funded with facts,
We can cite only two of his acts:
Begat Lamech, age one eighty-seven;
Age nine sixty-nine, went to heaven.

A Hard Voyage

Said God, "This contemptible race
Has proved itself shockingly base.
Such rascals! Confound them,
I fear I must drown them.
They're sinning all over the place.

"You, Noah, deserve to be saved,
For you're not even mildly depraved.
Build an ark. Make it huge,
To withstand the deluge,
Lest you sink to a watery grave."

Then Noah (his family, too)
Assembled an unabridged zoo.
"What a stench!" Noah cried,
Hanging over the side.
"Every one of them needs a shampoo."

Forty days, forty nights, how it poured!
They were itchy, rheumatic, and bored.
But they weathered the flood,
And debarked in the mud.
"Last one off is a slug!" said the Lord.

The Tower of Babel

The descendants of Noah
(Which no one was not)
All spoke the same language,
All dwelt in one spot.

They were building a tower,
It reached to the sky.
"I call *this*," said Jehovah,
"Egregiously high.

"They are inches from heaven.
The next thing you know,
They'll be right in our laps.
That tower must go!

"One has got to deal firmly
With people like these,
For they're apt to forget
Why I gave them their knees.

"I shall send them all packing—
They'll learn to obey!
Let their tongues be bamboozled!
Let babble hold sway!"

And that's why new languages,
Rich and complex,
Were invented by Frenchmen
And Urdus and Czechs.

An Unfortunate Incident

"Cursèd Sodom," God raged, "is an outpost of hell!
I consign it to flames—and Gomorrah as well."

Two angels, dispatched for the purpose, told Lot:
"Clear out of here fast, before things get too hot.
This cesspool called Sodom is doomed. You're excused—
Just don't ever look back. God would not be amused."

In a shower of brimstone and fire, Lot fled,
But his wife absentmindedly swiveled her head.
She was changed to a pillar of salt, Mrs. Lot.
I, for one, don't believe she deserved what she got.

Disaster Narrowly Averted

When Sarah, nearly ninety-one,
Bore Abraham an infant son,
They conscientiously revised him—
That is to say, they circumcised him—
According to the will of God,
Who doesn't like to spare the rod.

They doted fiercely on the child,
A fault that drove the Good Lord wild.
"Go, Abraham, and render me
Your dear son's life," commanded He.
"Your ardor has been misdirected.
Young Isaac must be vivisected."

"My Lord," groaned Abraham, "he's Thine!"
His ancient eyes filled up with brine;
And though the fearful edict crushed him,
He took the boy and neatly trussed him
And settled him upon a pyre.
He raised his knife. He raised it higher . . .

"Stay!" cried an angel. "Abraham!
God sends a sacrificial ram.
Cut Isaac loose, the trial is ended.
Your piety's to be commended."
Wept Abraham, "The Lord is good."
One hopes that Isaac understood.

Twins

Esau said, "I'm feeling faint."

"Aw," said Jacob, "no, you ain't."

"Papa's blessing," Esau cried,

"Is mine by rights. But I'll have died

Of hunger first. For pity's sake—

My birthright for your lentils, Jake."

"Your birthright?" Jacob murmured. "Sold!

Dig in, before the stuff gets cold."

Jacob's Ladder

Mused Jacob: "A singular dream!
That ladder! Those angels agleam!
And the Lord blessed my seed—
Which is just what I need.
What a boost for the old self-esteem!"

A Romance

Jacob fancied Cousin Rachel,
Uncle Laban's comely child.
Seven years he toiled to earn her,
While her glances drove him wild.

When at last his bride was bedded,
Jacob drew the veil to kiss her.
Under it was Cousin Leah,
Rachel's older, squint-eyed sister.

"Be not so distraught," said Laban.
"Though at first she looks alarming,
Leah's fun. I'll throw in Rachel—
All for seven years of farming!

"Only seven more, dear nephew,
For the pair. You find that shocking?
Rachel will divert you nicely,
Leah darns a dandy stocking.

"Take the two. And take their handmaids—
This, I think, is rather lavish—
Saucy Bilhah, nubile Zilpah.
Both of them are yours to ravish!"

Leah bore him seven children,
Zilpah had a couple more.
Rachel and her handmaid, Bilhah,
Managed yet another four.

One of Leah's was a daughter.
Sons made up the other dozen.
All twelve tribes of Israel sprang from
Jacob's craving for his cousin.

The Story of Joseph
(Mercifully Condensed)

"Come see my pretty coat," said Joseph.
"Papa gave me it."
"What horrid taste!" his brothers cried,
  And threw him in a pit.

  They hauled him out and sold him to
  A band of traveling men,
  Who headed south for Egypt, where
  They sold him off again.

  But Joseph landed on his feet.
  He found he had a bent
  For listening to Pharaoh's dreams
  And telling what they meant.

When, by and by, the folks back home
Turned up in Egypt's land,
How goggle-eyed they were to find
Their Joseph in command.

He greeted them affectingly,
And made a joyful noise,
Exclaiming, "Oh, my dear Papa!"
And "No hard feelings, boys.

"Come, Hebrews all, and pitch your tents
Beside the glittering Nile.
For I am Pharaoh's fair-haired boy!"
Said they, "The kid's got style."

Dispensation

Unless you like stats,
Just skip the begats.

On the Banks of the Nile

The daughter of Pharaoh
Was thrilled to the marrow
When Moses turned up.
(He was cute as a pup.)

Crying "Isn't he luscious!"
She snatched from the rushes
This child of the Jews,
Who would later make news.

Captivity

"Tell Pharaoh Jehovah proposes,"
  Said God, "that the Hebrews go free."
"You know, I st-stutter," said Moses.
"He'll never l-listen to me."

  Said Pharaoh, "It's out of the question.
  I won't be deprived of my Jews."
  Said Moses, "J-just a suggestion.
  But I'm glad I'm n-not in your shoes."

"L-Lord," Moses groaned, "it looks hopeless.
  He won't l-let loose of us Jews."
  Said God, "Then I'll plague him with locusts.
  The wretch is absurdly obtuse."

The Ten Commandments

"With the tip of my terrible finger I write
My laws on a couple of stones.
You, Moses, make sure you hold on to them tight,"
Said the Lord in implacable tones.

"They're heavy," groaned Moses. "And what if I fall?
I'll break *all* Ten Commandments at once.
No offense, but I wish you had written them small—
I'm g-getting too old for such stunts."

Heroism

The Canaanites, for twenty years,

Had punctured hapless Jews with spears.

The Israelites at last uprose

And slew their Canaanitish foes.

Bad Captain Sisera alone

Survived and, eager to postpone—

Or better yet prevent—his end,

Sought sanctuary with a friend.

Who wasn't in. His wife, Jael,

Cooed, "Captain, you're not looking well.

My tent is yours. May I suggest

A nap? Stretch out, take off your vest.

Perhaps you'd like a glass of milk?"

Her voice was soft as spider silk.

(Four lines that follow may offend.

If squeamish, skip and read the end.)

The villain slept. She tiptoed round

And nailed his noggin to the ground.

To guarantee that he was dead,

She severed the unsightly head.

"All hail, Jael!" the Hebrews sang.

"That varmint was too mean to hang!"

Gossip

"There goes that lunatic, Samson,
  Running off to his trollop, Delilah.
  The fellow just can't keep his pants on.
  Have you ever seen anything viler?"

Luck

Ibical-bibical,
Boaz of Bethlehem,
Single, respectable,
Very well-heeled,

Caught the attention of
Young widow Ruth, who was
Complementarily
Poor. But genteel.

Divine Retribution

When the Hebrews and Philistines fought to the death,
The idolatrous Philistine horde
Slew a great many Jews and, though quite out of breath,
Made off with the Ark of the Lord.

And His vengeance was swift, and His vengeance was hot.
"Alas!" they exclaimed. "How it smarts!"
For He smote them with hemorrhoids. Cruel, was it not?
They had rather been smitten with warts.

Epitaph

Here lieth
Goliath.

Nothing stopped him
Till David dropped him.

A Tribute

Of worthy Samuel I sing,
Who never (what a shame!) was King.
His task it was to find, appoint,
And with a drop of oil anoint
The Kings of Israel. He first
Selected Saul, a man accurst.
Undaunted, he chose David next—
Brave, charismatic, oversexed.
As far as anyone could tell,
The only flaw in Samuel
Was this: a tendency to shout
And flap his skinny arms about.

Bad News

Despondent and given to fits,
King Saul, at the end of his wits,
Was informed by a ghost
That the Philistine host
Would chop him, next day, into bits.

A Scandal

Uriah the Hittite's wife, Bathsheba,
Was as dumb and curvaceous as an amoeba.
Which is what prompted King Dave
To misbehave.

Justice Is Served

Pigheaded, wicked Absalom!
He tried to steal his father's throne.
(His father was King David, who
Had recently been wicked, too.)

Insolent Absalom! The fool
Rode off to battle on a mule.
He caught his head upon a limb;
The mule strolled out from under him.

Poor, hapless Absalom! In vain
His roaring, kicking, raising Cain.
He dangled, helpless, by his chin
Till someone came and did him in.

The revolution having failed,
One would expect that peace prevailed.
But David bellowed, overcome,
"Oh, how I miss my Absalom!"

Solomon Sings

True, my marriages *are* frequent
(As some people have complained).
I find foreign girls so piquant,
My miscegenary passions can't be reined.
                    Can not be reined!

Now, Egyptian girls are moody,
And Moabites are bold.
Jewish girls are goody-goody,
With a suffocating tendency to scold.
                    Oh, how they scold!

There's no doubt my lust's excessive
(Seven hundred foreign wives!),
But my stamina's impressive—
I've three hundred foreign concubines besides.
                    I said besides!

Time, I'm certain, will be gracious
When it tallies up my wrongs.
How, if I were less salacious,
Could I write my magnum opus, *Song of Songs*?
                    That *Song of Songs*!

A Bad End

Jezebel, King Ethbaal's daughter,
Practiced witchcraft, crimped her hair,
Worshipped Baal, wore too much makeup,
Drove Elijah to despair.

Sordid creature! Dogs devoured her,
Though the brutes, it seems, had qualms.
Several parts they couldn't stomach—
Skull, and perfumed feet, and palms.

Notes on the Prophet Elijah

Nobody cared to incite
Elijah, the hairy Tishbite.
When he called for a drought, it got dry.
When he called for a death, it was definitely goodbye.

He was fed by ravens.
He was fed by a widow.
He was fed by an angel.
Whenever he wanted to eat,
God sent meat.

Nobody crossed that prophet,
Though they yearned to yell, "STOP IT!"
He called down fire out of heaven and burnt up fifty-one men. Twice.
So nobody ever said, "Elijah's a tough son of a bitch but basically nice."

The Esther Story

High-handed Haman, esteemed by the King,
Did an evil, ignoble—nay, damnable—thing.
He proclaimed, "We have too many Hebrews by far.
Let them therefore be slain, in the month of Adar."
When the news reached Queen Esther, she shivered a bit,
Then cried: "Down, I say, *down* with this scrofulous writ!"

She invited her husband and Haman to feast.
When they'd guzzled their fill, and their chins were well greased,
Said King Ahasuerus, "Dear Lady, bravo!
What gift shall I give you, what trinket bestow?
What prize will you claim for those tasty ragouts?"
Said she, "Save my life! And my people—the Jews."

"Who threatens my Queen? What despicable hound?"
Esther pointed to Haman, who fell to the ground.
King Ahasuerus was horribly wroth.
His eyes were afire, his lips were afroth.
Very little remains of this story to tell.
Horrid Haman was hanged, and his ten sons as well.

The festival Purim, which Hebrews observe,
Commemorates Esther—her cunning, her verve.
They dress up in costumes, and sing jolly tunes,
And eat hamantaschen, a cookie with prunes.

Realism

Is the Book of Job

An attempt to probe

The question of why God made a wager with Satan at Job's expense?

Or is it meant to instruct us that, from a celestial point of view,

Whatever we do—or don't do—

The distance between God's understanding and ours is immense?

(Which is why Divine Justice doesn't always make sense.)

In either case, isn't it wise,

Given the vanity of mortal surmise

(Unless, perhaps, you are tempted by Job's dunghill?),

To do nothing so virtuous or so vile

That it prevents you from keeping a low profile?

Attract attention, you're going to foot the bill.

If Satan don't get you, the odds are God will.

Jonah

Jonah, the Prophet, reluctant to prophesy,
Fled from Jehovah and hid on a barque.
Found and flung overboard! Swallowed, spat up again!
Syria welcomed him well before dark.

Jonah, much chastened, made haste to prognosticate,
Fresh from the terrible lips of the whale:
"Forty days only till God destroys Nineveh!"
Causing the Ninevan public to quail.

Turning from sin, they repented repeatedly,
Praying and fasting and rolling in mire.
God spared the city and pardoned the populace.
Jonah was cross, for he looked like a liar.

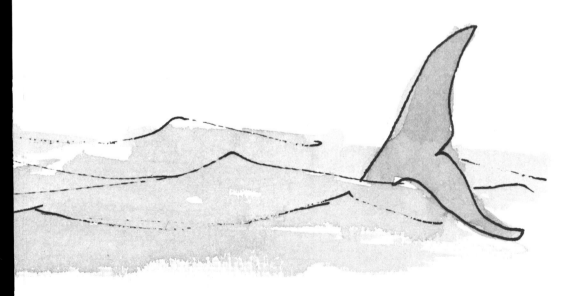

Minor Prophets

The prophets Habakkuk and Amos
Are considerably less famous
Than Isaiah or Jeremiah.
It's not that they lack fire
(The curse of any minor prophet
Can send a miscreant to Tophet).
But when they exhort,
They do keep it short.

Continuity

Our forebears (thanks to good King James)
Talked funny. They had oddish names.
They fell in love, succumbed to lust,
And trampled strangers in the dust.
They suffered flood and fire and drought.
A few of them remained devout.
Their lives were jolly, vapid, grim,
According to Jehovah's whim.
How little things have changed since then!
Whose fault that is, God knows.

                         Amen.